A Student's Guide to

Cloudstreet

by Tim Winton

Helen Parr
B.A., Dip.Ed.

WIZARD
BOOKS

First published in 1999 by
Wizard Books Pty Ltd
ACN 054 644 361
P.O. Box 304 Ballarat 3353 Australia
Email: wizard@netconnect.com.au
www.wizardbooks.com.au

ISBN 1 87636715 6

Cover design by Cressaid Media
Printed by Shannon Books, Melbourne

Quotations from *Cloudstreet* are reprinted by permission of Penguin Books and the author © Tim Winton 1991

Contents

Notes on the Author   5

Genre, Structure and Style   6

Summary and Commentary   11

Characters, Issues and Themes   28

What do the Critics Say?   42

Sample Essay   45

Essay Topics   48

NOTES ON THE AUTHOR

Tim Winton was born in Perth on 4 August 1960. He grew up experiencing what he has described as 'a quintessential Australian suburban life', complete with picket fence, Hill's Hoist in the back yard, and Holden in the driveway. Summers were spent at the beach (Scarborough Beach, not far from Karrinyup, where he grew up), beginning his life-long love of the sea. It is very much the world he describes so often in his fiction.

His father was a policeman, and when Tim was twelve, the family began to move to different locations around the state. A childhood insomniac, he often lay awake in the night. Sometimes he was able to hear through the wall what his father told his mother at the end of the day. These sometimes horrifying tales of accidents, murder and mayhem gave him an early acquaintance with the dark side of human experience, which certainly shows up in his stories. He was fortunate however to have loving parents and to enjoy a happy childhood. His essentially compassionate, family-oriented world view can be said to stem from these early influences. He was raised in the strict teachings of the Church of Christ, a fundamentalist Protestant sect which emphasises the importance of personal morality in each individual's life. Christianity introduced Tim to what he has called the 'big questions' (the meaning of life, the meaning of death, the nature of good and evil), and although he outgrew his childhood commitment to the church, he did not outgrow a deep-rooted Christian faith, nor an interest in the 'big questions'.

As a teenager, he began to write. Study at the University of Western Australia refined his talents, and he submitted his first novel manuscript at the age of twenty. It was accepted, and published, under the title *An Open Swimmer.* It jointly won the Australian-Vogel award (the most prestigious award for young writers) in 1981. Winton's subsequent work has been just as successful. *Shallows* (1984) won the Miles Franklin award (the most famous literary prize in Australia). In 1985, *Scission* was published, and in 1987, *That Eye, the Sky* (made into a film in 1995), with *Minimum of Two* and *In the Winter Dark* following in 1988.

The last three mentioned were written while Winton was overseas. He lived for two years in Paris, Ireland and on the Greek island of Hydra, before returning permanently to his home state. He now lives in a small seaside town 150 km north of Perth, with his wife Denise and three children. He describes himself as committed to life in a small town, and living by the sea. When not writing, he fishes, swims and surfs at the beach nearby.

As well as his adult fiction, he has also published two enormously successful children's books, *Lockie Leonard, Human Torpedo* and *The Bugalugs Bum Thief*. Meanwhile, his adult fiction has continued to be published. *Cloudstreet* (1991) won four awards: the Miles Franklin, again, the Banjo, the West Australian Premier's Award and the British Deo Gloria award. Winton has been described as the wunderkind (wonder-boy) of Australian fiction, given his prodigious output while still so young. If the critical reception of his work has varied from time to time, his public acceptance has not. His reputation as one of Australia's most important authors is firmly established.

THE TEXT IN PERSPECTIVE

GENRE, STRUCTURE AND STYLE

Genre

Cloudstreet is essentially a human drama, a novel whose focus is primarily psychological. It is a vast work, a saga or epic of sorts, as we follow the fortunes (and ill-fortunes) of two families, playfully named the Lambs and the Pickles, over more than 20 years. Our concern is largely with what befalls the characters and how they respond to the challenges of circumstance, or as Sam would say, the 'shifty shadow of God'. We follow the inner needs and demons of the central characters as they are played out, together with their individual and collective struggle to find meaning and harmony in their lives and to make sense of the tragedies that have been visited upon them. We are not invited to be preoccupied with the tragedies or ill-luck, but rather on what Winton's characters do with it. The contrasts between the two families, as they are brought together by chance in the one ramshackle house (with its own tragic history) provides much of the tension and interest in the novel. As the story develops however, our attention is drawn more to the individual stories of the key characters – Fish, Quick, Rose, Dolly, Oriel and Sam – until the very end where the notion of family and community prevail.

Cloudstreet is identifiably Australian. Winton evokes the beauty and desolation of the Australian bush, the burgeoning postwar city of Perth, and the Aboriginal sense of space and place (and at various points contrasts that with the Lambs and the Pickles' feeling they don't belong in Cloudstreet). He is suggesting there's an important lesson to be learned from Aboriginal Australians. Indeed, Winton makes much of the question of place, of belonging (or the need to) and the importance of community (see Themes). More obviously, Winton's language is Australian as he invokes the colourful old Australian working class vernacular ('whakko the did', 'I'm flat out like a lizard drinkin', etc). In part this is consistent with the time in which the novel is set. In another way, it reflects on the inarticulate, almost anti-intellectual view of the characters. Mostly it seems to capture a time gone by, a nostalgia for something simpler, though not necessarily easier. One suspects Winton has great affection for this now almost lost Australian idiom. We don't say 'blokes' anymore do we? We say guys. We don't say 'Fair dinkum!?'; we say 'Really!?'. Winton celebrates a language that no longer has currency. And this is true of much of his work.

While Winton seems to strive for naturalism in his portrayal of the characters, there are surrealistic elements or perhaps what might be described as magic realism. Inexplicable things happen (a pig talking in tongues to Fish, Quick coming back from the bush 'glowing like an Osram lamp'). Yet we are invited to somehow believe in them, because such moments have spiritual meaning for those characters and a way of making sense of a chaotic world. Winton combines the real with the magical in a seamless kind of way. Although some readers might resist this juxtaposition, or question its success, it does add to the appeal and charm of the novel.

Structure

The novel opens with a kind of prologue, although Winton doesn't title it as such, in which we see scenes of happy families, of life and fertility, narrated by someone, we know not who. We aren't given any names or other reference points to help us understand who these characters are and why this scene is significant. It is not until the end of the text, or perhaps well into the text, that we come to understand the point of this 'prologue' and its larger meaning in the text, and to understand that these first few pages are in fact set in the present (the '60s) while the rest of the story takes us back in time, until we come full circle in the last chapter.

Cloudstreet is a rambling text, ambitious in its scope, yet it is also highly structured. Following on from the opening scene, it is organised chronologically, from the early 1940s through to the '60s, (apart from one scene in Chapter Three which takes us back in time to the history of the house itself, Cloudstreet – an important flashback which establishes many of the key concerns of the text). The effect of this structure is to create the sense that we are watching things unfold; we are in the position of wondering what's going to happen, of hoping for them, of trying to predict outcomes, and much comes as a surprise. The writer and the narrator are in control here and we are drawn along on the journey.

The story is organised into ten chapters, each one moving us forward not only in time but in the development of its characters and thematic concerns. For example, Chapter One focuses on the Pickles, a dysfunctional family down on their luck; Chapter Two introduces us to the stoic, God-fearing Pickles and the tragedy of Fish; and so similarities and contrasts are established. Chapter Three brings the two families together in the house, Cloudstreet; Chapter Four focuses on the tensions between the families. With each chapter we are taken further into the secrets individual characters hold within themselves and their sometimes fumbling attempts to exorcise them or come to terms with them. Some might describe the ending as neat, perhaps even sentimental, as characters make choices we are invited to see as personal growth and as loose ends are tied up. We see resolution and a degree of harmony by the end of the text, echoing the joy and harmony described so beautifully in the first few pages on the text. The ending brings us back to the beginning.

It is also highly structured in another interesting and unique way. Winton entitles 'episodes' within each chapter, and in doing so he offers a taste of what is to come as if we are witnessing key scenes in the lives of the individual characters in each family. Each title either signals a key event (for example, 'Fish Lamb comes back'); is revealing of a theme ('Stickability') or keys you into a particular character's state of mind. ('Quick Lamb's Sadness Radar'). You won't necessarily be conscious of this as you read, as you immerse yourself in this huge story, but in another sense these 'signposts' guide you through the text.

Style

Stylistically, Winton's language is playful, vital, passionate and often original, as he creates new words to capture an image or feeling. Of special interest is the way he moves from everyday Australian idiom to poetic, almost mystical passages that reflect on the wonder and meaning of existence. This is achieved through his use of shifting narration; he moves from the gritty, often humorous, dialogue of inarticulate characters to the apparently all-knowing Fish, visionary in his understanding of the families' problems and his own. These shifts often take the reader by surprise and we begin to understand at these moments that it is Fish (or the other part of Fish) who, surprisingly, is the narrator of the story. It is the narrator who provides the insights into the characters' inner lives, as they cannot express what it is they know because they can't find the means or words to do so.

Much of the writing is witty, some laugh-aloud funny, and this is indeed a part of *Cloudstreet*'s charm. What's more, the humour is glimpsed at some of the darkest moments in the text. Consider the description of Sam having his fingers torn off in a cruel accident. Against expectation, they're described as dancing 'like a half a pound of live prawns' on the deck. We feel anguish and smile at the same time. At other times, the drama of the Lambs and Pickles is punctuated with delightful scenes of of child-like behaviour, such as when we see a young Red Lamb take her revenge on 'perving' boys at the local pool, as she urinates on their 'awestruck faces...She could pee through the eye of a needle Red Lamb'.

Symbolism is a very important part of the novel's style and meaning. The central metaphor is the river, 'the beautiful, the beautiful, the river'. This reference to the famous old Christian hymn symbolises the dreams of people who look to the 'other side', the next life, to be rewarded for what they haven't had in their mortal life. It represents the spiritual source of enlightenment. The river is literally where some of the main events happen – Fish's near-drowning and hungering to return; scenes of Fish and Quick's brotherly bonding are on the river, Rose and Quick's finding one another occurs on a boat on the river and scenes of family unity and joy are set beside the river. It is where healing takes place and where characters figure things out. This is contrasted with the claustrophobia of Cloudstreet, of Rose's dismal workplace, of Oriel's retreat to her tent. Winton is concerned with the healing powers of the natural landscape, the sense of place and of open spaces. It comes across in much of his other work (*An Open Swimmer, Shallows*) represented in these scenes and those featuring Aboriginal Australians. Even the names of the characters have symbolic meaning: Fish, because that's what he wanted to join; the Pickles, a sidedish to the productive and solid Lambs; Dolly, a woman harking back to her girlish youth; and the Lambs and Pickles together in Cloudstreet, like a counter lunch – though the union, promised, is a long time coming.

SUMMARY
AND COMMENTARY

Shadows...

Prologue

An unnamed narrator is describing happy families picnicking by the river, eating, drinking, carousing, swimming. We understand the narrator is in fact a part of the scene 'Will you look at us by the river?' We shift to the third person narration: 'He hears nothing but the water...'and we see someone savouring the idea of jumping into the river and leaving this happy group behind.

Chapter One

The Pickles – Sam, Dolly and their children, Rose, Ted and Chub – live in Geraldton, with Uncle Joel in the Geraldton pub. The war is still on. Sam has a job on a boat, mining guano for phosphate. We learn that Sam's father was a water diviner, and had taught Sam to believe in luck, or as he called it 'the shifty shadow of God'.

Sam, a gambler at heart, had grown up on the racetrack. His father had wanted him to be a jockey and Sam, who loved this "soft sentimental man", recalls the night he found his father dead beside him. The dream to be a jockey died with his father.

On this particular day at work Sam feels the "shifty shadow of God lurking" and knows he shouldn't get out of bed. Rose, his daughter, back in Geraldton, also feels something is going to go wrong on this day. Sam goes to work on the boat. There is an accident and Sam loses four of his fingers in a winch.

Rose meanwhile discovers Dolly, sleeping with an American soldier in the pub. Sam is brought back to Geraldton and Dolly is a reluctant visitor at the hospital, seeing the accident as simply yet another piece of bad luck for her. Sam decides the one thing he can do now is fish; he joins his brother Joel on a fishing expedition and Joel suffers a heart attack.

Commentary

This first chapter establishes the Pickles as a family down on their luck. More importantly, we see both Sam and Dolly as almost fatalistic in accepting the unpredictability of life, or destiny. (This becomes more significant later in the novel as the contrast between this attitude and those of the Lambs is established.) We also see that they are not united as a family: Dolly spends her days in the pub, drinking and picking up men, trading on her good looks for a sense of worth and sexual power. The animosity between Rose and Dolly is palpable, especially in the scene at Sam's bedside, but there is a genuine affection and love between Sam and Rose. Even at this early age young Rose is the organiser of the family, cast unwittingly into the mother role that Dolly appears to have abandoned, and providing emotional support for her hopeless but lovable father.

In many ways this chapter is about lost dreams – Dolly's hankering for dreams of sexual freedom as a girl, Sam's past dream of being a jockey and Rose, a girl bitter about shouldering responsibilities we understand shouldn't be visited on someone so young.

Chapter Two

Now we are introduced to the Lamb family, who live in the bush. A family of six – Lester and Oriel, and their children Mason (Quick), Samson (Fish), Hattie, Lon and Red – they appear comfortable and happy in one another's company. We are told everyone loves Fish, for his wit, alertness and cheeky good humour. The Lambs are a poor family but devout. Oriel is used to making do and proud of it.

Lester takes the two boys out prawning at night and tragedy strikes. Fish is caught under the net. Quick realises he is on the net that is trapping Fish. Oriel, from the shore, knows something is terribly wrong. They drag Fish in and Oriel, with fierce effort and determination, and prayers to God, brings Fish back from the dead. Rejoicing they take him into town. But Quick realises as he cradles his brother that 'not all of Fish Lamb came back'.

Commentary

Unlike the Pickles, the Lambs are a united family who do things together. It becomes clear that Oriel is the mainstay of the family. Lester, though a good father, is a bit slow at both farming and policing.

The scene of Fish's drowning and near-death is perhaps the most dramatic and poignant scene in the novel, as we imagine the horror of his entrapment, witness Quick's guilt and Oriel's urgent and furious efforts to revive him. However it is Winton's description of Fish drowning that suggests that at some point Fish embraces the water, in a sense swimming down towards his death in a way that is strangely beautiful and moving, almost mystical. Contrast this with the description of Fish's reaction to being revived by Oriel: '...pain and the most awful sickfeeling is in him like his flesh has turned to pus and his heart to shit. Shame. Horror. Fish begins to scream'. It is not the river, a giver of life and sustenance, that has taken Fish, but human error and endeavour. The consequences of his being revived, and changed, are to reverberate throughout the whole novel and have terrible effects on Oriel (ironically, his 'saviour') and Quick.

Chapter Three

The chapter opens with a brief description of the tragic history of the house, Cloudstreet. We learn that it was owned by a widow with missionary zeal but little humanity. With the encouragement of the local priest, she briefly used to house young Aboriginal girls who had been taken from their families. Upon the accidental death of one of the unhappy girls, the widow cruelly evicted the rest of them. She died suddenly soon after, and it was not until some time later she was found by the priest.

Having had it unexpectedly bequeathed to them by Uncle Joel in his will, the Pickles arrive at Number One Cloud Street. It is huge but run down. Rose explores the house. What money they had also inherited was gambled away quickly by Sam. Dolly feels out of place, without the identity she had in Geraldton. Sam divides the house in two and advertises half of it for rent. Soon after the Lambs arrive, and despite misgivings about it looking 'haunted', they set about making it liveable and productive.

Oriel sets up shop, 'Lamb Smallgoods'; this is in direct contrast with the inactive Pickles. Quick sticks up pictures of the war-wounded, the miserable, on his bedroom walls and declares he hates himself. Lester invites an Aboriginal man into the house but he runs away, sensing something very wrong.

Oriel and Lester take Fish off to a doctor, who declares there's nothing physically wrong with him. Fish will not emotionally recognise his own mother. 'He just looks through her like she's not there.' Oriel reveals to her daughters her family background; the fact that she brought up her stepmothers' children when her father remarried, and because of this missed out on an education and the opportunity to become a teacher (as her stepmother was). She also tells them about the half-brother she loved and help raise, who was killed in World War One. Dolly is disgruntled, drawn to the railway tracks. The chapter finishes with the end of the Second World War.

Commentary

The terrible history of the house is in part a reminder of the tragedy of what is now referred to as 'the stolen generation' of Aboriginal children.

We are told that the 'house was boarded up and held its breath'. This explains the Aborigine who, after visiting Cloudstreet, ran away from the house. Winton is effectively making the house itself a character in the novel – it has its own past and its own identity. He suggests that Aboriginal Australians are alive to the spirituality of place. Rose too is overcome by a 'hot nasty feeling' when she enters that particular part of the house.

It is also a scathing attack on sanctimonious 'do-gooders' whose charity is a form of self-glorification, rather than the natural expression of compassion. Winton gives us some neat 'justice' in the sense that the widow died soon after, her hard bony nose stuck on middle C; this sound is to be significant later in the novel.

The differences between the two families are also suggested symbolically in the house, which 'took on a wonky aspect', suggesting the idea of imbalance. It also emerges in the difference between Dolly and Oriel. Dolly being drawn to the train tracks evokes her desire for escape, while Oriel sets up a business, something solid and productive.

In contrast to the women, Lester and Sam share an unspoken understanding of each other's grief, despite their differences. Perhaps the most poignant moment in the chapter is the scene with the doctor – Fish's refusal or inability to 'see' Oriel is not only a torment to her but a reminder of what Fish really wants, to embrace the very thing that Oriel stole from him. Fish doesn't blame Quick; in fact he is closer to him than anyone else.

Chapter Four

The chapter opens on a happy note for the Pickles, aptly titled 'Break in the Weather', as Sam gets a job at the mint and wins on the races. This is contrasted with the description of Quick's 'sadness radar' as he reads thirstily about dead soldiers and observes the poverty of the McBrides at school. Soon after, Quick is also a horrified observer of Wogga McBride's death when he gets run over by a train. Lester uncharacteristically lectures Quick about his withdrawal into himself and his ignoring Fish. Oriel reflects on what she sees as the hopelessness of men. They 'lacked flint'. Her sorrow lingers over her stepbrother's death in the war. Sam takes Lester to the races and a little of Sam's recklessness rubs off on him. The animosity between Rose and Dolly intensifies and Rose declares to herself that she hates her mother, and 'hated being alive'.

The Lambs go fishing and we see Fish joyous in this scene with his brother by his side. Fish speaks of his longing to join the river.

Dolly's family background is revealed: her sister was really her mother. Rose finds her drunk and passed out beside the railway tracks, but having found her, leaves her there. Oriel looks after the alcoholic Dolly and cleans up the Pickles side of the house, much to Rose's shame. The Lamb's pig talks to Fish; Lester hears it, but Oriel doesn't. The chapter ends on New Year's Day 1949, with Oriel moving out of the house into a tent in the backyard.

Commentary

' Cloudstreet ticked but didn't go off.' In this chapter there is a focus on the tensions between characters and within individual characters.

The Wogga McBride incident is another reminder of the fickleness of fate. It cruelly echoes the 'death' of Fish: a boy watching his brother die, as Quick in a sense also did. What is Winton suggesting here? That the world is random, dangerous and without meaning? The existentialists and other modern thinkers have argued that life is accidental and unpredictable, and individual alone in the face of its indifference. This seems to be emerging as a view in Winton. Lester's admonition of Quick, about getting on with things, with life, accepting the way Fish now is, comes straight after this scene and one senses the author here, admonishing us all to 'get on with it', to embrace life, despite its injustices and horrors.

We now begin to get a larger sense of Fish as the central character and as narrator; he speaks to Quick, to himself, and of course to us, directly. He is also in some ways an embodiment of the transcendent, the magical, the sublime. It is he who hears the breathing of the house; he is the one in spiritual contact with the tormented past residents of the house, and it is he who communicates with the pig. In contrast is Oriel who, when taken down to 'hear' the pig, can't (just as Fish can't see her). We feel for her, but she is so closed off to the magical, the absurd, the impossible, that it somehow all makes sense. Curiously, it coincides with Oriel beginning to question her long-held religious beliefs, though there is no suggestion of either a questioning or a hankering after Christianity. Her moving out to set up camp, as it were, in a tent, is symbolic of both a seige mentality and at the same time, a compromise of sorts – perhaps her own curious way of giving herself time to understand what's happening to her and her relationship with Fish in this strange house that 'breathes'. It might also be interpreted as defeat, but for Oriel this could only be temporary.

This chapter is also about change and fluctuating fortunes. Despite Sam's luck, the Pickles are no happier. Rose is beginning to withdraw further, as Dolly deteriorates into alcoholism. Up to this point it has been hard to feel much sympathy for the embittered Dolly, but a brief hint at her family background gives a sense of why she is competitive with her own daughter and contemptuous of other women. Oriel's efforts to help the 'poisoned' Dolly and clean up the Pickles side of the house is well-intentioned but intrusive, though Oriel in her no-nonsense, practical way probably wouldn't understand Rose's injured pride and fury at Oriel's gall and her 'help'.

Chapter Five

Three or four years have passed. Quick is sixteen. After a brief talk with a teacher at school about real misery and history, the annihilation of the Jews and Hiroshima, Quick no longer feels the need to punish himself. He decides to leave and tells his mother simply, "I'm going", without explanation or discussion. Fish sinks into a depression and 'calls' to Quick. The pig no longer talks to Fish.

Oriel's response to Quick leaving is to move into action and she competes fiercely for business with a GM Clay, but it rebounds on her as she puts him and his family out of business, which shames her. We learn that GM Clay is Dolly's lover (Sam is told of this by Mrs Clay). Rose's developing anorexia is observed by all, most notably her father and Quick, and her 'intensity' at school frightens off potential friends. Sam makes a half-hearted attempt at suicide and Rose is the one who is there to help him. Rose's compassionate observance and love for the soft, beautiful Fish is expressed in this chapter. Rose is also beginning to confront her mother; she tells Dolly she's going to love her own children. Rose gets a job as a switchboard operator and discovers 'she really can talk'. She also begins to grow 'flesh on her'. Oriel recalls her past, the loss of her family in a fire and how she 'grew steel in her' as a result. Ted Pickles 'shoots through', with little explanation. The chapter ends with Lester and Fish in a kind of communion, Fish smiling.

Commentary

This chapter exposes us to the manifestations of the characters' inner turmoil: Rose's anorexia; Sam's near suicide at being made to confront Dolly's infidelities and his own inadequacies; Fish's depression at Quick leaving; Oriel's shame at her competitive response to the loss of Quick; Dolly sinking further into alcoholism and her pathetic attempts to hold on to some semblance of youthful sexuality.

However, while there is reason for sadness, in the desertion, separation and loss depicted, there are also some positive and cathartic aspects. Quick's leaving, we later discover, has a healing effect on him; and Oriel recognises for herself that what she's done is morally wrong (Mrs Lamb weeps). More importantly, Rose begins to awaken. The discovery that she can speak, represented in the job she gets, empowers her as if she's awakening from a long sleep. We feel that this sensitive girl is about to unlock some of her demons.

Chapter Six

The entire chapter explores Quick's time away in the bush and his physical and spiritual change. He kills kangaroos to eat and to sell and one attacks him. While passed out, Quick has visions of Fish calling him to move. An old farmer finds Quick, unconscious. Fish calls to Quick. On recovering, Quick is signed up to kill kangaroos to protect the nearby farms. During this time, Quick has visions of himself running. He meets the farmer's daughter, Lucy, and has his first sexual experience. They are caught at night together, naked. Driving away, Quick picks up an Aborigine in a pinstripe suit, laden with bread and wine, which he shares with Quick. Quick feels the desire to tell this 'blackfella' all about himself, but doesn't. He just keeps driving, guided by the man, until to his surprise, the Aborigine asks to be dropped off right near Cloudstreet.

Quick drives away quickly and ends up back at Margaret River where he gets a job as a pig driver with his father's cousin for a year. In a moment off work, Quick goes fishing at the scene of Fish's accident. He catches vast numbers of fish, as if they are literally throwing themselves onto his hook. At this moment of real happiness, Quick has a vision of a black man 'walking upon the water'. He keeps having visions of himself and of the black man and is found by his relative 'lit up like a sixty watt globe'. They drive him back to Perth.

Commentary

Quick's escape from Cloudstreet works on a number of levels to illuminate some of the ideas Winton is exploring. First, the manner in which he does it, highlights his (and other characters') inability to express feeling and to explain to themselves or others what drives their actions. Secondly, the very places he ends up (because his journey is depicted as a subconscious drifting, as if other forces, or destiny is guiding him) represent the stages and important moments in Quick's life to this point. The episode where the silent Aborigine 'guides' him to Cloudstreet is heavy with religious symbolism, as indeed is the image of a black man, god-like, 'walking on water'. He breaks bread and drinks wine with him in a kind of silent communion and is led to the very place – Cloudstreet – he wants to escape. The notion of fish multiplying as it were when Quick is on Margaret River is a direct reference to the fishes and loaves episode in the Bible. Quick being 'illuminated' suggests very strongly that he has 'seen the light' as it were, or undergone a conversion; 'he saw everything in the headlights, every-damn-thing'. It is almost as if Winton is suggesting that this could only come from being in the bush – in communion with Nature – and more significantly with Aborigines who, in some strange, unspoken way, enlighten Quick. Quick doesn't analyse or articulate what the visions mean. Neither does the narrator. We are left to understand that it is a matter of faith and the intangible, all-important spiritual aspects of our existence.

Chapter Seven

This chapter opens with a scene of Fish's happiness and, once again, the pig is talking to him. Hat gets married. While Fish keeps a vigil at Quick's bedside (he is still seriously ill after his episode in the bush), Oriel and Lester discuss the meaning of what happened to Quick. Oriel expresses a loss of faith and a sense of having 'lost her bearings'.

Sam is in trouble with bookies and Lester takes him to a shack out of town, to hide and wait it out. Lester visits Dolly to let her know and she begins to seduce him. Lester, after the initial shock, is eagerly co-operative. Lester returns to Sam with the money for Sam to pay his debts but Sam convinces him he can win the money. Lester ruminates on his own shame and losses, and his stupidity at having let Sam convince him. We also see Quick having conversations with Oriel and then Lester which are more reflective and contemplative about life. There is a brief scene where we see Rose and her 'other life' outside Cloudstreet, as she writes in her diary about a date.

Oriel takes in a woman called Beryl Lee, whose husband has deserted her. She is a hard worker but is also something of a righteous busybody. Later in the chapter, a number of the characters comment on observing Beryl 'fading'. Beryl informs Lester she is leaving and intimates it's because she has 'feelings' for him but that she is going to 'marry' the church as a nun.

Oriel takes Quick prawning and surprises him with her insights into his feelings about Fish. She also asks him to help her understand herself. Immediately after, Oriel and Quick catch a bounty of fish (despite the fact that as Quick says, 'it's not the season'). The chapter finishes on a further happy note as Sam wins in a big way and the family feast on the catch of prawns.

Commentary

There are subtle but real changes in the life of the Lambs and Pickles, a growing sense of them healing and trying to articulate their inner feelings. Quick, after he recovers from his 'glowing', seems more stable and happy to be back with his family, as indeed Fish is happy. Oriel is a little less stoic and more questioning. The scene where she and Lester talk about the meaning of things is important. Oriel openly expresses her acceptance of the 'strangeness' of things and her loss of faith. She acknowledges 'the real war' – the one within herself. This is echoed too in the gentle scene between Oriel and Quick where she asks him if she's been a good mother. Contrast this with her earlier sureness and tendency toward action rather than reflection. Oriel doesn't usually ask questions; she answers them! Certainly we are invited to see this as a positive sign. Lester and Sam, despite their differences, make it known to one another that they understand each other. Lester too is depicted as questioning life and wondering what's it all for. One of the episodes, entitled 'Wakings', is evocative of this broader theme. Fish tells his brother 'Everyone goes', suggesting both the idea of change and of acceptance of death, the ultimate transition. The recurring motif of the river and the Biblical symbolism of the fish is once again underlined. The questioning and reflection takes place on the ever-present river and the joyous catch of fish occur here too.

The inclusion of the character of Beryl is curious. One wonders if she is there simply to underline some key themes of the novel. Beryl's aloneness contrasts starkly with the centrality of family as it is depicted by Winton (despite its losses and sorrows). Her 'fading' is a direct contrast with Quick's 'illumination' and it takes place when Quick returns (as if balance has been restored). Quick is embracing the family and Beryl is leaving for a form of isolation – the nunnery. Just as chapter five deals with loss, this chapter could be said to explore notions of struggling to understand loss. While most of this chapter deals with the Lambs, there are also positive signs for the hapless Pickles: Dolly is described at one point as 'sober' and there are also hints of Rose's growing sociability and sense of self. The fact that the end of the chapter shows us Dolly embracing Sam and the Lambs feasting on the prawns (instead of selling them) is a direct contrast to earlier behaviour, leaving us with a sense of healthy (and long-awaited) change.

Chapter Eight

Rose is now twenty-four. She meets Toby, a hack journalist, through her job on the switchboard. While we learn she has been out with other men, she is virginal and self-conscious. Initially, Rose is defensive about their different backgrounds, as he introduces her to a different world – conversing with Toby's intellectual, artistic friends, eating in Perth's ethnic restaurants. He writes poetry in his spare time, which Rose privately regards as 'drivel'. While Rose believes she is in love with Toby, it is clear that he doesn't see her as his equal. When Toby does get a poem published, they attend a 'do' at the editor's house. However, it soon becomes apparent that they have the wrong man and it's not Toby's poetry that has been accepted.

Stung by wounded pride and desperate to cover the mistake and amuse the literati, he publicly humiliates Rose, referring to where she lives and the 'slow boy' and the 'lady in the tent. She runs off,

SUMMARY AND COMMENTARY

heading towards the river, where Quick and Fish find her crying on
the riverbank. Quick is now a self-employed fisherman. She joins
them in the boat and in amongst the exchange of banter Rose suddenly asks 'What are you like, Quick Lamb?' to which Quick replies
'I reckon I'm tryin to figure out what I lost.' He tells her his whole
life has to do with Fish. Rose finds peace and calm on the river with
Quick and Fish and unexpectedly asks Quick what they'd be like
married. When they arrive back at Cloudstreet, they make love, 'with
a surprise that turns to recognition'. Both sets of parents react with
shock, but the chapter ends with their wedding and Oriel dancing
with Dolly, as 'turn by turn something grows'.

Commentary

The brief excursion Rose takes into a wider, middle-class world
she didn't know existed seems at first to be offering her satisfac-
tion. But significantly, this world is rejected. Winton, through Rose,
seems contemptuous of the literati with their 'Englishy accents' and
intellectual posturing; they are portrayed as pretentious and shallow.
Rose's honesty, home-grown wisdom and sharp wit is shown in
revealing contrast with Toby's job as a gossip columnist, his patronising attitude, his 'ugly and nonsensical' poems about sex and his
hypocrisy in embracing the bourgeois scene he had earlier criticised.

Rose running away and joining Quick on the river is very
symbolic. We're told beforehand that everything important that happens to Quick happens on the river. Quick's 'Dad and Dave' style of
speech is not mocked but rather presented as an appealing contrast to
the meaningless, superficial 'drivel' of Toby, just as Toby's cruel
treatment of Rose is contrasted with Quick's gentleness. We also see
Quick articulate for the first time in saying how significant Fish is in
shaping his life to date. Quick and Roses' coming together is amaz-
ingly sudden and the explanation offered to the reader is Rose saying
to Quick 'I know you all of a sudden'. The suggestion is that it was
meant to be, but previously obscured by the traumas and pain they
had in their own individual ways been through.

Their union symbolises the union of the two families, represented most obviously in the final scene where Oriel literally and
metaphorically embraces Dolly (who, importantly, does not resist).

The reception is in an RSL hall, a homely but happy affair (which we are invited to compare to the sumptuous but frigid place Toby took Rose).

In this chapter the all-knowing Fish as narrator recalls how Rose once loved him and, like a premonition, cautions her (or us?) about Toby, a man with 'his tongue in your ear and cheese on his chin'. Fish's need to return to the water, or as he sees it 'the stars', is emphasised in this chapter and it is significant that he is with Quick and Rose when they 'find' each other. The effect of this is to further underline his centrality as the character most in touch with feeling (he knows 'the house hurts') and, ironically, in creating harmony.

Chapter Nine

Rose declares to Quick that she wants to live somewhere new, where people haven't been before. To finance the move Quick tells her that he will become a policeman, 'to fight evil'. Upon his graduation, Rose tells him she's pregnant and he responds joyously.

Sam wakes to feel the 'hairy hand of God' upon him once more. Dolly is attempting to sober up but, ironically, falls and breaks her leg. At the hospital Lester and Sam agree that their respective wives are 'too much' for them to handle. Two deaths follow – Ted dies (in a sauna, trying to lose weight to be a jockey, like his dad wanted to be) and Rose miscarries. Dolly is distraught at the news of Ted's death, declaring 'he was the one I loved...He was the one' and gives up on sobriety. Rose lapses back into anorexia upon losing her baby, and the silence of surburbia is beginning to get to Quick (it's made clear he misses the restlessness and noises of Cloudstreet). Sam, feeling the weight of sorrow about Rose and Dolly, hears Fish thumping the walls next door. He sees the ghost of the old woman who died in the house and Sam tries to comfort Fish, who cries at the woman who 'won't let him play' the piano.

Rose is hard and bitter and rejects Sam's impassioned request to help him look for and help Dolly. Dolly is found and it is evident that she has allowed herself to be sexually degraded and possibly abused. Rose is 'forced' by Sam and Quick to visit her in hospital. She declares how much she hates Dolly for stealing her 'innocence', 'trust' and 'childhood' from her. Dolly begs her to come back and see her and Lester advises her to 'go on with [her] life love. It's all there is'. Rose returns the next day to see Dolly. They talk without recrimination and an unusual degree of honesty and openness as Dolly tells Rose 'you should never trust a woman'. She then tragically reveals that her sister was her mother. This scene ends with Rose and Dolly embracing and weeping together. This is a turning point. Dolly sobers up and Rose falls pregnant again.

The Nedlands murders, a random and cold-blooded series of killings (a real episode in Western Australian history), intrude at this point and act as a catalyst for Rose; she gives into Quick's idea to return to the 'sanctuary' of Cloudstreet. We are given graphic descriptions of the Nedlands murders. Yet the murderer upon capture is seen to be a 'frustrated man with a hare lip…and a lifetime of losing'. His capture coincides with Rose giving birth in Cloudstreet (with Oriel at her side), to Wax Harry. The chapter finishes with a description of the way 'the house breathes its first painless breath in half a century'.

Commentary

This chapter is filled with tragedy and death, – but also birth, rebirth, and renewal. There are new beginnings. Rose and Dolly find an opening, the beginnings of a real relationship. It is significant that this comes only after the death of Ted, and of Rose's baby. Those deaths prove cathartic for both, as Rose confronts her anger and Dolly confronts her demons. In the process, we see a softening and mellowing in each character. Winton has been criticised for the neatness of this plot design, yet on another level it seems we have been waiting for the moment when mother and daughter would find a way through to communicate.

Throughout the chapter the presence, or ghost, of the 'blackfella', mystically appearing at critical times and advising Quick (such as about not moving into the new home) is contrasted with the evil that Quick wants to fight and the evil of the Nedlands murders. There is evil in 'orderly, calm suburbia', while it is suggested that there is wisdom and peace in the spirituality of Aboriginal culture and sense of place. At one point it is even suggested that Oriel might have been a victim of the Nedlands murderer had it not been for a 'a man with black arms akimbo' appearing, and ironically, the squealing of Fish's pig.

Equally underlined is the importance of fertility and family as a way of countering the emptiness of the womb, of isolated suburban life, and of death. In Sam's speech to Rose about the centrality of family one can feel the author speaking: 'You can bear it when you lose money and furniture. You can even grit yer teeth and take it when yer lose your looks, yer teeth, yer youth. But Jesus Christ when yer family goes after it, it's more than a man can bear'. It is fitting, and no doubt symbolic, that Rose gives birth in Cloudstreet, surrounded by family, rather than in the sterility of a hospital.

The notion of a balance being restored by the benign and life-giving elements is highlighted. At the birth of Wax Harry, 'the spirits on the wall are finally being forced on their way to oblivion…freeing the house, leaving a warm, clean sweet space among the living, among the good and hopeful'. It almost feels like a happy ending when Dolly announces with pride 'I'm a grandmother. Good night'. Yet there is still one more important thing to be resolved, as we see in the final chapter.

Chapter Ten

Harry's birth brings a degree of contentedness and harmony to Cloudstreet. Elaine comments on how much Rose is like Oriel. There is a passing reference to the Kennedy assassination but in the next sentence we are told 'Cloudstreet sweetened up like a ship under full sail'. With the death sentence pronounced on the Nedlands murderer, it is Oriel who is horrified at Quick's glee. She tells him it's barbarism and runs out of the room. Lester tells Quick (and us) that it is Oriel's life's work to believe in 'love thy neighbour as thyself'. Fish, as narrator, tells Oriel, who is 'still waiting for answers that don't come', to 'Wait'. It has the feel of an omen. Quick is too late to save a drowning boy, who turns out to be the son of the Nedlands murderer and in a moment of clarity and reflection later tells Rose 'there's no monsters, only people like us'.

Fish as narrator tells us that with the house clear of evil spirits, his turn is coming. A black man meets Sam on voting day, and tells him 'Places are strong, important'. We are also later reminded that

Aborigines at this time still don't have the vote.) Soon after, Dolly indicates to Sam that she doesn't want to change or sell Cloudstreet. There is a gathering of both families and Oriel cooks up a feast the night before Quick and Rose are due to leave on a holiday. It is a harmonious affair, and Dolly and Oriel find themselves agreeing on a number of things. Rose and Quick take Fish with them on their holiday, at Rose's insistence. The descriptions of Harry, the baby, and Fish, the man, are disturbingly similar. The urgency of the all-knowing Fish to 'feel whole and finish what was begun' is made strikingly clear.

Out in the middle of nowhere, under the stars, Rose reveals a change of heart (and personality?) as she tells Quick she doesn't want to be independent, she wants to be her with people, her 'tribe' at Cloudstreet. Rose and Quick return home early, announcing in a celebratory fashion that they're staying in Cloudstreet. In the last scene 'Moon, Sun, Stars', Fish describes the two happy families picnicking by the river, and we're reminded of the opening scene of the novel. Fish embraces the river and completes what was begun a long time before. The scene of his drowning is exultant.

Commentary

The notion of coming full circle, of completeness, is the dominant theme of this chapter. Quick comes to an understanding that we know Oriel already has, that it's not 'them and us', it's just us. He finally accepts himself, enjoying a feeling of absolution over the matter of Fish and an ebbing of his suffering.

The idea that a life without meaning, familial connection and personal striving can lead to 'evil' is also suggested. It's a Christian notion, though one comparable with principles of modern psychology, and it permeates this chapter, if not the entire novel.

It is interesting to observe how Rose has in a sense become an Oriel – embracing family as the answer to happiness and inner calm and as strong and dominant in her new family as Oriel has been. The religious symbolism is strong once again – the feast of the Lambs and Pickles is evocative of the feast before Jesus died. Just as Jesus knew what was ahead of him, so too does Fish.

The metaphor of the river, traditional symbol of life and continuity, is once more a key element to note. The celebration of Cloudstreet takes place by the river, in what is a union of two families. Even more radical is the matter of Fish's drowning, beautifully evoked not as a tragedy but as a moment of wholeness: 'Being Fish Lamb. Perfectly. Always.' The other part of Fish has been waiting a lifetime for the 'rest' to join him. And if we weren't sure before, we certainly know now that Fish has been the all-seeing narrator, signalled in the words 'as long as it took to tell you this'. He had to wait for his time to come again, until there was unity in Cloudstreet, and so a kind of unity for him in death.

Epilogue

The novel ends with Oriel and Dolly. Oriel is unpegging her tent and Dolly crosses over to the Lambs where a fence had once been. Together they fold the tent and return to the open-doored house.

Commentary

After Fish's death, the 'walls' (metaphorically and figuratively) have come down. Oriel is no longer trapped in a seige mentality. Dolly is helpful and accepting of the woman who once stood for all she hated. It is interesting that the novel ends with the two mothers, once so divided, now in a kind of silent union. It is appropriate that two women who have suffered the painful loss of their most loved ones, are the ones we see at the end. Their being together is a potent symbol of unity in Cloudstreet. We already understand that Sam and Lester have an understanding of one another and we are led to believe that Rose and Quick have a life together ahead of them. The door is now 'open' in Cloudstreet, in marked contrast to the early claustrophobia and sense of not belonging that marked the earlier parts of all characters' dwelling in Cloudstreet.

WHAT DOES IT ALL MEAN?
CHARACTERS, ISSUES
AND THEMES

CHARACTERS

Fish

The character of Fish is multilayered. He is the narrator of the story, a character in the story and symbolic of much that Winton explores in *Cloudstreet*.

On one level, Fish is an intellectually disabled boy (and man) who responds to people and events purely on an emotional and intuitive level. He senses Rose's misery as a young girl; he is unable to acknowledge Oriel because at some level he knows she is responsible, through 'saving him', for his living death. He is extremely close to Quick and 'calls' to him when Quick heads off to spend time in the bush. He is also, arguably, the character most connected to the spiritual aspects of human existence, as evidenced through his capacity to communicate with the spirits of the dead. He is connected too, to the natural world: his 'talking' to the pig, but more significantly his connection to the natural landscape, the 'moon, sun and stars' and 'the beautiful, the beautiful, the river'. He is all these things paradoxically through his disability.

The 'other side' of Fish however is the omniscient narrator with insight into the other struggling characters, more of an observer than a participant. Compare the descriptions of how Oriel had begun to dress him as an idiot and (in Chapter Ten) how Quick notices his flabbiness and helplessness, with those of Fish, as articulate narrator, evoking the beauty of a simple, harmonious family scene in the prologue and many other moments in the text. Winton's use of the shifting point of view from outside narration where we are told about Fish, to Fish the poetic, all-knowing narrator, takes the reader by surprise at first. We hear the other voice of Fish – 'What are you thinking Fish? Do you feel like you're going, you're close?' – talking directly to him. Then just as suddenly, there's a shift to "I" in the first person; 'I travel back to these moments to wonder at what you're feeling...You're coming to me Fish...' (p 403).

The idea of Fish being stuck in between life and death and the wider theme of needing balance, redress and harmony is potently symbolised through Fish and Fish's plight. It is as though he is 'outside' the mundane concerns of ordinary people – in touch with the life force as if seeing it clearly, and also in touch with death. He is present as the catalyst for much that happens, notably Oriel's loss of faith and Quick's guilt. He is also an absence – from his mother, but most particularly from being who he should or could have been. His connection with death emerges not just at the beginning and end of the novel, but when he communes with the spirits of Cloudstreet and speaks as one with the ghostly, inexplicable appearances of the blackfella.

When his death comes finally, we see it as release, not a tragic suicide. Through the novel, we hear of Fish's need to get back to who he was and could have been. There's a strong element of being invited to celebrate his release from this world, just as we find joy in the opening scene where we're told that 'he' for 'a few seconds' will 'truly be a man...and he'll savour that healing all the rest of his journey', when he dives into the river. When the families in Cloudstreet have struck some kind of harmony (notably achieved through Rose and Quick's union and the birth of Wax Harry), Fish can let go and find himself, 'Being Fish Lamb. Perfectly. Always. Everyplace. Me.' In Fish, Winton implies that death is part of life – mysterious, even frightening – but ultimately resolved in the joys of the living, which have the power to cancel out its darkness.

Rose

Rose's journey is a torturous one. She believes her mother hates her and she declares she hates her mother. She is thrust into a role of looking after the family at too-early an age – finding Dolly when she's 'gone off the rails', dispensing advice to the lovable but weak Sam and making sure there's dinner on the table for all the Pickles. She has seen and experienced too much. She struggles to establish an independent role for herself but without real success. Her response to this struggle, in developing anorexia, is practically a disappearing act, as it were. This response to her family situation and personal circumstances in lamentable but understandable.

Yet she is anything but a passive victim. Throughout, there is a strong sense of her will, her indominitable spirit. She keeps to herself, loving the boy next door (Fish) because he is beautiful and because she understands suffering. She immerses herself in books to escape the reality of her life but this aspect of her character also suggests that she is intelligent and sensitive to language, despite her not talking, her prolonged silences. We understand that Rose is able to communicate in very eloquent, and sometimes blunt, ways (with Sam most notably) but often chooses not to.

Her independence begins with her finding a job, symbolically as a telephone operator, where she must talk, albeit anonymously, and it is here that she finds her own voice: 'Rose suddenly discovered how to talk'. In this way she can forget the problems of her family life, have a sense of independence and spread her wings a little. It is through this job that she meets Toby, a well-intentioned, but ultimately hypocritical, weak young man. She knows this about Toby early in their relationship, privately disapproving of what she sees as the pretentiousness of his poetry, and we too are invited to see it that way. Her ultimate rejection of the middle-class literati, in a sense forced upon her as she escapes Toby's attempted humiliation of her at a party, is a turning point in Rose's growth as a young woman. That she is drawn to Quick in the following scene, almost as if it were meant to be, signals her embracing something (and someone) simpler, more honest than the flashy but shallow Toby. That she 'discovers' Quick who was 'under her nose' the whole time represents an awakening of sorts in Rose: 'I know you all of a sudden' she tells him. Rose's sudden proposal to Quick is in keeping with her characteristic instinctual and emotional responses and her capacity to get straight to the heart of things, apparent earlier in her conversations with Dolly and Sam, respectively.

Rose is a survivor and intelligent, able to analyse what's happening around her and within her. She is the only other character, apart from the omniscient Fish, who demonstrates the ability to really articulate both thought and feeling. In the following scenes, despite the setback with her first unsuccessful pregnancy (and concurrent, though temporary, relapse into anorexia), we see a more confident Rose. This is underlined most particularly when Dolly reveals the truth about her past. Rose is able to forgive and to understand, and the scene in the hospital between mother and daughter tells of Rose's growth as a human being and her compassion. She mellows to the extent that her anger, at the world and her mother, begins to dissipate. With that comes the birth of her first child. She is a conscientious mother, one who has a lot more in common with Oriel than with Dolly. Rose will be the kind of mother Dolly could never be, though not in a competitive or obsessive sense; she will be, because Rose believes in family, her 'tribe', a trait she shares with the well-meaning though dominating Oriel.

Rose has experienced much: she has been largely unprotected from life's battles; she has struggled through a debilitating disease; she has experimented a little with life outside Cloudstreet and she chooses in the end to embrace what family can mean. Some readers may feel that Rose has chosen a predictable domestic path over other possible options; others will feel that Rose's choices are right and natural – a sign of deeper wisdom and attachment to what is really meaningful.

Quick

Quick's life is overshadowed by the burden of guilt. He knows Fish was the favoured one and feels that he was solely responsible for Fish's near-drowning and subsequent disability. This guilt colours his growth for most of his young life. He cannot escape it, nor can he express it or share his burden. This inner turmoil is signalled in his tendency to dwell on the misery of others, as he covers his walls with pictures of the prisoners of war, refugees and other victims of circumstance. Quick's 'sadness radar' reflects his need to punish himself for what happened to Fish as he feels it should have been him. His witnessing the violent death of Wogga McBride parallels his own presence at Fish's 'death' and underlines Quick's being drawn inexorably, as if he were a messenger of death, to tragedy. That Quick suffers low self-esteem and arguably, a tendency to escapism, rather than action or reflection, is not simply because of

Fish; this is signalled earlier, before Fish's tragedy. He was the 'slow one' of the family thus ironically called Quick.

Quick is in some ways, the archetypal, inarticulate male, struggling to make sense of life without the vocabulary or intellectual equipment to understand its absurd and tragic complexity. However, his sensitivity and compassion distinguish him from the likes of Ted and Chub, who are ignorant, unself-conscious Australian males without Quick's finer qualities. Indeed, Quick is highly self conscious, a characteristic he shares with the young Rose.

Quick's time in the bush is likened to a religious awakening as he comes home 'glowing'. From this point in the novel, we see a young man, grown to accept Fish as he is and one who now has plans to 'fight evil' as a policemen. This is in direct contrast to his earlier immobility and passivity. His marriage to Rose completes a picture of Quick, as he finds, without consciously searching, a happy ending for himself.

Oriel

Oriel believes in hard work as a means of salvation. Her response to tragedy (she doesn't believe in 'bad luck', in direct contrast to Sam and Dolly) is to act, to produce, to keep on going. At an early age, she 'grew steel in her' to cope with whatever life brought. She is stoical and soldiers on the face of adversity. She tells Lester in a reflective moment about the need for 'keepin' yer head above water... War is our natural state.' We also learn early on that her family is 'god-fearing'. This Christian woman seems to embody the very Protestant notion of work, of getting on with things, making the very best of poverty and sharing what little you've got.

It is ironic that she struggles to hold on to her faith after Fish's refusal to acknowledge her and then later, Quick's sudden departure.

Oriel is admirable, but she is not a character that we warm to quickly. She is bossy and at times intrusive. Her cleaning up Dolly and the Pickles' household (including Rose's room) is well-intentioned, but we are invited to see it as Rose does; Rose is humiliated at Oriel's lack of sensitivity to others and other ways of seeing the world. Her retreat to the tent can be seen as just that – a retreat. However, she hasn't given up or given in. She still runs the family, the business and remains the stalwart matriarch.

There are moments later in the novel when we see Oriel question what it all means, what life is about. But she comes to the conclusion 'that everything can be helped', eschewing any idea that you can't control your fate. She is still fighting for the miracle (presumably the restoration of Fish in some way) so she can get on with the 'real war', the one we're led to understand is within her. This scene with Lester is one of the few times we see Oriel speak about her needs as a human being and even then she cannot fully articulate what she feels or believes in. Her need to belong to something (a family, a place, a religion) is perhaps stronger than that of any other character, possibly stemming what she lost as a young girl – her mother, being supplanted in her father's attentions by a step-mother who denied her the chance of an education, and the death of her beloved step-brother.

With Fish's final release, we see a woman being assisted by Dolly to fold up the tent, suggestive of the notion that she has resolved a part of that war within her. Perhaps it's symbolic of her acceptance that it was right for Fish to go; and hinting at that, she still has faith in her God and faith in the second commandment, 'love thy neighbour'.

Dolly

Our first impression of Dolly is one of a selfish, adulterous and hard-hearted woman. Her response to Sam in hospital is to think of her bad luck in being tied to such a 'loser' and this comes straight after we know she has been in bed with an American soldier.

Yet it is Dolly's yearning for something better in her life that prevents us from condemning her outright. We realise that her alcoholism and bitterness have a source, and we sense this justification or cause long before we are told details. We find out that her family background was a tragic one; her sister was in fact her mother. She has internalised this knowledge and comes to hate women, trusting in the arms of the men who desire her; later even competing with her own daughter. At sixteen, we are told, Dolly was already 'out on her back under the night sky with a long procession of big-hatted men'. She came to equate approval with sexual attractiveness. Her sense of worth is embedded in sexual conquest, even when she knows the liaisons to be loveless and hollow (recall her brief sexual encounter with Lester).

There is more to pity in Dolly that to condemn. Despite her affairs, we also get a strong sense of her loving Sam, almost against her will. Through much of the novel, Dolly is hopelessly harking back to a youthful past where she was desirable and things were carefree and possible. She is drawn to the railroad tracks, symbolic of her desire for escape, just as she escapes being a responsible mother and escapes into the bottle when reality bears too heavily on her. It is no wonder she can't stand the likes of Oriel. While she feels superior to the almost asexual, bossy woman next door, there is too a degree of envy of someone who appears to cope so well with the circumstances of life.

In the end, Dolly is a character who appeals to our understanding and compassion. She is not repugnant, despite her obvious failings. This is most poignantly evoked in the hospital scene where she tells Rose about her long-held secret. It is a turning point for Dolly. She desperately wants to be a good grandmother and to make amends with her daughter. The 'big blowsy woman' joins Oriel in the final scene, acting to help mend the 'gash' between the families and within her.

Sam

Sam is a fatalist, a believer in the 'shifty shadow of God', a view on the world he inherited from his father, Merv, the water diviner. Sam is also a gambler, which perhaps fits the notion that 'hairy hand of God' can strike you lucky or lead to a 'life-long losing streak'. In this way, Sam is, as Rose and Dolly surmise, 'hopeless', because he doesn't believe in creating your own 'luck'.

However, he is generous of spirit, forgiving and loving. He tries hard to excuse Dolly's adulteries and her meanness because he has a capacity, however ineptly expressed, for understanding and compassion. He tries to make Rose happy too and he understands her needs; the scene where after Sam's winning streak Rose comes home to find books, pens, and a desk waiting for her, is telling of his attempts to be a good father. When Rose develops anorexia, Sam tries to force her to eat and then to make jokes ('bag a lettuce leaves?'). His language is often colourful, and witty. Sam tries to fill the void created by Dolly and his deep love and concern for Rose is made abundantly clear.

While Sam seems to submit to Dolly, to fate, he is also an optimist, ever-hopeful that the wind of chance will change in his or their favour. The scenes where he eggs Lester on to have a drink and a punt at the races (and as Lester observes he doesn't look like a loser in this context) are full of life and fun. The contrast between uncertain Lester and lively Sam underline Sam's capacity for life. He is the loveable larrikin, redeemed not simply by his stumbling but compassionate efforts with Rose and Dolly, but because he lacks any maliciousness or bitterness, because he is slow to blame and quick to find the good in people, something he shares with the good-hearted Lester.

Lester

Lester feels he doesn't measure up: to Oriel, and to expectations of what a good man should be. It's made clear early on he wasn't a particularly astute copper, and only a cook, not a soldier, at Gallipoli. He feels overpowered by the pragmatic Oriel but he is grateful to her for loving him. His feelings of inadequacy however don't get in the way of his being a good father and man. In a conversation with Quick, he likens himself to CJ Dennis' 'Sentimental Bloke'; and this in part sums up Lester. He just wants to be loved and to love. He helps bind the family together, he creates the fun and games they play (like the spinning knife) and he hankers after a vaudevillian career as an entertainer.

Lester is in the background much of the time and we are not offered a lot of insight into his character. However, it is his voice at critical moments that dispenses wisdom to the self-absorbed Quick as he tells him to shake himself out of his self-imposed exile and misery and to think of Fish. One can't help but agree with him. Later it is also Lester who urges Rose to see her mother in hospital: 'Go and see her, love…I can't stand the hate. It'll kill you…Go on with your life, love. It's all there is.' (p.353) Some readers might see this as simplistic, home-spun wisdom but there's a sense in which it is astute and hard to disagree with. The soundness of Lester's advice is later reinforced when we do see a reconciliation between Dolly and Rose. While our focus is on other characters, notably Fish, Quick and the three female characters, Lester comes across as a complex, though somewhat unrealised, character.

Ted and Chub

Sam and Dolly's two sons are only incidental to the storyline. They are marginalised characters but they also serve a function in terms of highlighting problems within the Pickles' family. Unlike the Lambs, who always seem to be together, or trying to be, the Pickles' family (five in all) are not a group. This highlights the differences between the two families. The brothers add little support or apparent understanding of their sister, father and mother. They also serve to emphasise the blokey inarticulateness that Winton repeatedly explores in the novel.

Ted has more significance in terms of the plotline because Dolly's favouritism of him (over Rose), is noted early on and is central to understanding Dolly's character ('never trust a woman') – something we understand only later. Ted harbours sexual feelings about his mother. His death, trying to lose weight to be the jockey his father never was, seems somewhat contrived, as it is this that leads to Dolly's almost total breakdown and the important confrontation and reconciliation between Rose and Dolly.

THEMES

The need for communication

Winton playfully embraces Australian idiom, and creates his own, almost as if he is paying homage to a language that is almost lost, by adding to it. It's colourful and expressive language. However, it often obscures some deeper feeling. It's the antithesis of the more contemporary (and American?) notion of unburdening one's individual thoughts and feelings as therapy and in order to find the truth. The characters do know things; they just can't find the words they need to express what's inside them.

Winton seems to suggest that the holding of secrets and a lack of communication is ultimately damaging. This is true of many of the characters, as they attempt to repress their feelings and react in ways which block possible expression. Consider Oriel's setting up her tent in a futile attempt to deal with her feelings about Fish; Quick's abrupt and non-communicative withdrawal into himself and his inability to explain why he needs to leave; Rose's anorexia; Dolly's holding onto a terrible secret about her past. There are also the monosyllabic utterances of Ted and Chub that highlight an unhelpful aspect of male culture; the lies Toby tells himself; and other individuals which repeatedly express this theme in the novel.

It is only when the characters begin to unburden themselves, each in different ways and contexts, that we see the beginnings of something approaching a kind of healing. Dolly's late confession to her daughter (and perhaps to herself) about her past is cathartic (cleansing); Quick choosing to confront Oriel about her feelings about Fish signifies a positive change in him and his relationship with Oriel. It is the telling of their own stories, their own narratives that moves them forward. Perhaps Winton is suggesting that we all need to tell our own stories to grow and to heal wounds. There is also the non-verbal communication that seeks to heal. The scene at Quick and Rose's wedding where Oriel and Dolly dance together, looking 'so bloody proud', is a moving and profound moment in the text, just as the scene of both families feasting together at the end and beginning of the novel represents a kind of communing that is open and honest.

The centrality of family (or tribe)

There is little doubt that Winton celebrates the importance of family. When it is depicted as 'going wrong', we see the negative consequences of this. In Oriel, Dolly and Rose's childhood there was no loving and protective mother, and Winton makes it plain (reading between the lines) that this is what largely causes their pain. What is interesting is that the father figure is depicted in each of these characters' lives (and Sam's) as the loving and loved one. One may read this plot design as highlighting the absolute importance of the mother

CHARACTERS, ISSUES AND THEMES

in a child's life; it might also be interpreted as a bias on Winton's part, as it is the women who are most often portrayed as failing in what is the ultimate emotional responsibility.

There is a variation on this theme in the history of Cloudstreet the house. It is tainted by the spiritual presence of Aboriginal girls who were removed from their families and the consequences of this are tragic. As if in extension of the crime committed by the authorities responsible for the 'lost generation', the widow's actions are another betrayal. The subsequent suicide of one Aboriginal girl in her misery, and the widow's eviction of the rest are (theoretically) the very reverse of family caring and nurturance. As contemporary readers, we are able to draw on our knowledge in assuming that these girls were unlikely to be reunited with their families. The shadows that reside in the walls of Cloudstreet remind us about the importance of family.

Most obviously we have two families living side by side for twenty years, each with their own problems and secrets. The Lambs operate as a family; the Pickles do not and in the early stages of the story, the contrast between the noisy, communal Lambs and the silent, divided Pickles is starkly drawn. The images of the Lambs doing things together is suggestive of how families should be. Although individual characters in the respective families struggle privately with their own problems, it is only really when there is a sense of family unity that there is happiness, as exemplified in the river scenes with Lester, Quick and Fish, and of course the opening scene.

The marriage of Quick and Rose helps to create harmony within the two families and between them. The birth of Harry drives away the evil spirits of Cloudstreet, and is symbolic that a new life in the family literally and figuratively breathes new life into the families at Cloudstreet. Finally, the fact that Quick and Rose choose to stay at Cloudstreet amongst family rather than live separately, further reinforces the notion that belonging to a 'tribe' is what really counts. Some readers may see this as an overly sentimentalised vision of family. Others may rejoice in Winton's portrayal of people choosing harmony and unity over self-indulgent, strong individualism.

Place and belonging

The exploration of a connection to place is characteristic of much of Winton's work. The fact that Cloudstreet 'breathes' (with the ghosts of the Aboriginal woman and the widow) conveys the idea that places take on the spirit of the people who have inhabited them. 'You shouldn't break a place. Places are strong, important...Too many places busted,' the black fella tells Quick (and us).

Winton borrows from or embraces an Aboriginal notion of spirit of place and it permeates the entire novel in differing ways. When for example Oriel feels she doesn't belong in Cloudstreet, she moves out; she can't and won't compete with a 'living, breathing house'. Thus the notion of belonging and place are established as interdependent.

The claustrophobia of Cloudstreet and the encroaching city is contrasted at various points with the natural landscape, to suggest that real thinking and healing goes on in the natural environment. Quick's time away in the bush, and notably his connection with the blackfella (who one presumes understands the importance of place) leads to his illumination and enlightenment. His union with Rose occurs on the river, just as all the happiest scenes occur on the river, including most particularly Fish's eventual drowning, a return to where he belonged. Even Dolly's being drawn to the tracks evokes a notion of belonging somewhere else. Winton's depiction of the Australian landscape is much more loving than his descriptions of the urban environment. Contrast the evocation of the river with Rose's workplace, or the 'do' she attended with Toby, or indeed the inclusion of the deaths of Wogga and the victims of the Nedlands murderer; symptomatic of urban living?

Spirituality, fate and religion

The text is rich with references to religion and spirituality. Christian symbols abound. Consider the scene where the loaves and fishes are literally jumping into Quick's boat: t his is an allusion to Christ's miracle, and it happens, significantly, at a time when the individual characters and families are beginning to heal. The notion of a kind of last supper between the Lambs and Pickles just before

Fish jumps into the river, knowing and embracing his destiny (just as Christ did in the last supper), leads to a strengthening of faith, perhaps 'the miracle' that Oriel had been waiting for. The luminescence of Quick after his time in the bush is reminiscent of the period Christ spent in the wilderness, and it is the time of his awakening (the notion of 'seeing the light'). Oriel, who feels her faith slipping away from her, wants to know what he 'sees' because she is not in touch with spirituality. Sam believes in the 'hairy hand of God', and acknowledges God in his own fatalistic way. While the Lambs (as in the lamb of God) are 'god-fearing', so too is Sam 'god fearing' though not in any highly religious or church-going way.

Winton combines Aboriginal ideas of spirituality with those of European established religion. The ubiquitous blackfella reappears at critical moments in the characters' lives with understandings that are meant to enlighten them (and of course us). Sometimes he is a felt presence, at other times he physically leads characters (notably Quick) to their happiness. There is also a strong suggestion that Aborigines live in a very spiritual place, while the faceless cities (with their white atrocities committed against black Australians) have a different and inferior soul. The idea that white Australians have much to learn from Aborigines is a strong concern of Winton's. Some readers might find his using Aboriginal culture in a magical, mysterious way a little patronising, as if the realities of their oppression are absent (apart from the one episode when we are told the history of the house). Others may find a degree of enlightenment in his vision and see it as an important reminder about the original inhabitants of this land.

Beyond these references is the idea that we all need to find meaning in life; through religion, fatalism, the Dreamtime. There is no one answer it seems. The point is we all need to question, just as Oriel does. The answers might be found simply in the struggle, the desire to grow through experience, through being open to possibilities, and not being closed down to the inexplicable and the absurd.

The question of balance

The name of the horse and the hotel Joel owned, Eurhythmic, means 'harmonic structures' and this idea of balance has a lot to do with the position of the narrator, Fish. He needs to return to the 'other Fish', to achieve oneness, balance. This theme can also be seen in the history of Cloudstreet; the cruel widow suffered for her sins in her absurd death, a justice of sorts. Further, the fact that when new life was born into Cloudstreet it achieved balance; 'The spirits on the wall are fading, fading, finally being forced on their way to oblivion, free of the house, freeing the house, leaving a warm, clean sweet smell space among the living, among the good and the hopeful.' (p384)

In part, the question of balance has to do with good and evil and Quick is the character most in tune with this. Through the Nedlands killer he understands, through Oriel's teaching, that good and evil exist in every person. 'The murderer's wife. A man's wife. A man with evil in him. And tears and children and old twisted hopes. A man. With evil in him.' The killer was just one person who let the evil slide out. There seemed no reason. And yes we know he was duly punished for his heinous crimes. But we are reminded by Oriel: 'Killin' is men's business....not God's'.

So what are we to make of this – that there is a balance in the universe – good and evil; bad luck and good luck; life and death? Perhaps we are left in the end with the idea that it is best to see life in an almost yin and yang way – dark and light, weak and strong – and to see the balance between these opposites as crucial to order and stability. The author implicitly advises an active, flexible and humble mindset. It is the striving, the questioning, the hopeful, the forgiving, those who embrace life, rather than succumb to it, who finally endure and even flourish.

WHAT DO THE CRITICS SAY?

There's no doubt that Winton can write marvellous prose. It can offer wonder and delight...It's a kind of Australian *Under Milkwood* shading in and out of the Bible which allows for lovely rhythms and images that catch the heart and mind...Because he's writing about people who are inarticulate, slow-witted, untrained in thinking...and essentially languageless, Winton has to do it all for them. He can't ever narrate anything involving thought rather than mystery through their own perceptions. He has to tell us about it. This is perhaps what makes his characters at best archetypes and at worst stereotypes, living out certain myths of the Australian psyche, living through physical horrors....but not learning, changing, developing. It is to go on spiritual journeys whose end is to see the light that was always there, rather than to grow within yourself.... Sometimes the language is cruel: Winton looks at his characters with a cold detached eye and is never squeamish in his similes: 'She goes down the stairs with arse over, slopping more than she thumps, like a bag of yesterday's fish.' This kind of nastiness towards his characters I found unpleasant; there's no trace of love in it, and indeed despite its claims I often found this a loveless novel.

Marion Halligan, *Australian Book Review*

The language used in *Cloudstreet* was often full of so much love for the characters that Halligan's comment that 'Winton looks at his characters with a cold detached eye' appears totally invalid. Consider the section which describes a sad, regretful and defeated Oriel, that was in my opinion, truly beautiful and emotive : 'By the embankment, as the trains swept by, Oriel Lamb wept the sounds of a slaughter-yard and the grass bowed down before her...Rose saw Mrs. Lamb come blubbering down the street. Crying. Like a person. Mrs. Lamb crying. Rose saw her fall against the gate grabbing Fish who didn't move, who just looked across the road where no-one was, straight as a board with his mother's arms around him. Oh, it hurt to watch, even after the surprise, it hurt to see.' It is sections like this that make *Cloudstreet* strike me as one of the most loving, beautiful books I have ever read. The language manages to evoke strong feelings of sympathy and pity for the characters and the predicament they found themselves in, without wallowing in obvious sentimental prose.

Stephanie Saravanja, Year 12 Literature student, Victoria

Reading Tim Winton's *Cloudstreet* is like catching a wave.....the reader is caught up in the surge of Winton's powerful understated prose and propelled forward: it is an exhilirating ride. And then something goes awry. Characters that had charmed turn into disappointing stereotypes; the Australian vernacular winningly employed at first, comes to seem laid on by a trowel...the reader is unceremoniously dumped into the shallow water of melodrama.....One must hasten to add that this is not the sum total of his writing in *Cloudstreet*: there are numerous felicitious descriptions of the natural world – mud flats, rivers, wheatfields, the dog-days of summer – and behavioural nuances are also beautifully observed..

Kate Jennings, *Sydney Morning Herald*, March 30 1991

Tim Winton's latest novel is a big rollicking, ambitious work that moves along with a joy and exuberance sometimes matching the force of his beloved ocean. *Cloudstreet* can on occasion, with the sheer exhilaration of Winton's descriptive power, deliver the same sort of a disabling shove decent swell can exert, and yet, in all its unfolding and vibrant enormity, its great aimlessness, it can also leave you looking out to the horizon, wondering when the tide is going to change, wondering where all this water is leading to.

Catherine Ford, *The Age*

Tim Winton's new novel has barely hit the bookshops and already is being tipped for some of the top literary prizes. A saga of two families...it is full of comedy and tragedy, conflict and resolution. *Cloudstreet* contains much that is memorable – punchy dialogue, brilliant descriptions of the city and the seashore, vivid recurring images. ...At 31, Tim Winton is already recognised as one of this country's best writers. His prose has a wonderful clarity and simplicity. He creates a sense of place – particularly of his native Western Australian coastline – with stunning force. And he articulates the hopes, dreams, frustrations and triumphs of the solitary, battling families who people his land.

Judith White, *Sun-Herald*, 7 April 1991

The characters are charming, full of life and I found the experience of reading the text an enlightening, heart-warming, inspirational experience....It was an enjoyable, magical, uplifting experience.

Emma Dicarrodo, Year 12 Literature student, Victoria

A SAMPLE ESSAY

The characters' failure to understand or confront the source of their problems is what contributes to much of their sorrow and sense of loss.

To what extent to do you agree?

In <u>Cloudstreet</u>, the main characters struggle to make sense of loss in an absurd world. The road for most is long and hard, but ultimately they find something to hold on to. Despite their emotionally impoverished start in life, and/or the meaningless burden of tragedy visited upon them, each, in his or her own faltering way, finds shelter and meaning. Certainly, many of them avoid or have not the talent for self-examination, but was it their fault? How do any of us make meaning out of random tragic events, of feeling unloved, of losing someone dear to us, or simply of knowing we have missed out on life's chances? All of the characters have suffered. Through the often heart-wrenching story of the Lambs and the Pickles, Winton poses those big, aching questions: How does anyone deal with the often treacherous hand of fate? What are we to make of our lives?

Dolly is a prime example of someone who hides from the truth. The misery of her family background and sense of having missed out on something more are too painful to face. In looking for something to ameliorate her pain, she finds a kind of numbness or solace in loveless affairs, and the oblivion of alcohol. She is all too ready to apportion blame for her unhappiness on Sam, on Rose and even on Oriel. Underneath this bitterness at the world is a woman desperate to hang to the one thing she believed meant something – her good looks and desirability. She knows that these evasions provide no real answers, but is in fact a form of self-destruction. It is not until Ted's death that Dolly has her own awakening, confronting Rose with her past and facing her demons at last. She sobers up and determines to find an identity as a grandmother, a recognition both of her failure as a mother and desire to redress the balance, and an acknowledgement that she does in fact belong to a family.

Paradoxically, Oriel looks too hard for answers. She is hurting from her past losses and most potently the loss of Fish, her favoured child. It is much to lose but she, like Dolly, searches for something to make sense of it all, especially when her faith appears to desert her. Oriel asks questions, but finds silence. She tries to understand the absurd rather than accepting it. However, this begins to change as she talks with Quick, openly acknowledging the source of her pain. It's also evident when she finally embraces life. 'Let's do it right for once,' she says in the penultimate chapter, about their picnic arrangements, indicating a willingness to let go, to be frivolous, lavish. Just as Dolly moves from apathy to being more responsible, so too does Oriel begin to let go and we understand that these are, respectively, emotionally healthy responses to their inner pain. When they do open up, neither is particularly eloquent in their revelations, but that isn't the point. At least they confront their problems, and act on their new-found self-knowledge.

Neither Sam nor Lester pretend to have the answers, yet they keep trying. This is indicative of a desire to confront, rather than negate or deny the painful realities. Further, each in their own stumbling ways, tries to keep life moving inside Cloudstreet. They don't dwell on their problems but neither could it be said that they try to avoid them. Although equally inarticulate, they soldier on. They sense the problems in their families (in Lester's case, how to cope with Fish's inability to recognise Oriel and Quick's guilt, and in Sam's case, Dolly's apparent refusal to play the role of wife and mother and his daughter's anorexia) and quietly seek to better the situation. The fact that their interchanges and their dialogue with others is not peppered with elegant phraseology does not signal a lack of awareness and understanding.

Of all characters, Fish is the most complex. Dwelling in two worlds, the all-knowing Fish seems to have the answers for himself and his family. His knowledge is spiritual, intuitive and apparently all-encompassing. Fish most of all, ironically, is the most eloquent (despite being the character least able to directly communicate as a retarded young boy and man). This conjunction, and the two sides to Fish, is where we see some of Winton's most beautiful prose and insights. As the sad, retarded Fish, he does express his feelings, notably when he calls to Quick, and as the 'other' Fish he expresses what he knows to be the problem with Cloudstreet. At the end, he acts, going back to the others side in what is the ultimate personal confrontation, not sacrifice, and certainly not denial.

Rose, alone among the other characters, does have the means to verbalise her plight. Her clever, sometimes cynical, largely accurate assessments of her family and those around her, are striking. Yet, if anything, her intuitive union with Quick is more important, for it symbolises something central to the novel's argument. Winton suggests that growth and self-knowledge do not necessarily come from psycho-analysis and endless introspection but through feeling, through simple expression of truths when people are ready to do so. These may be simple, inarticulate working class people, but that makes them no less equipped to know the sources of their pain and with support, able in the end, to act upon the forces that could destroy them.

In the final analysis, the characters are redeemed not by thinking but by feeling, not by books but by family. Winton suggests that hard-won wisdom, love and the simple desire to search for a source of happiness are more likely to reap rewards than cold intellectual examination. He isn't being anti-intellectual in doing so (one need only to recall his descriptions of Fish's perceptions and Rose's astute reflections). Despite some criticism arguing that intellectualism and feeling are diametrically opposed in <u>Cloudstreet</u>, I think the reader is offered a much more interesting idea – that a failure to try to make some meaning out of your life ultimately leads nowhere. Perhaps we're left with a feeling that what is most important is to be aware, to be alive to the pain, however difficult that may be. Out of that confrontation, with the support of family, and in intuitive fulfilment of the human capacity to heal and grow, comes solace, if not happiness.

ESSAY TOPICS

Topic 1
'Fish is not only the narrator of *Cloudstreet*, he is also the hero.'
To what extent do you agree?

Topic 2
'In *Cloudstreet*, Winton suggests we have much to learn from Aboriginal spirituality and sense of place.'
Discuss.

Topic 3
'The narrative structure of *Cloudstreet* it its greatest strength.'
Discuss.

Topic 4
'Winton presents a setimenatlised version of aspects of past Australian society.'
To what extent do you agree?

Topic 5
'*Cloudstreet* suggests that the individual problems will be healed by being connected into a family.'
Do you agree?

Topic 6
'It is the Lambs, not the Pickles, view of life we are invited to see as positive and rewarding.'
Do you agree?